Introduction:

The book presents essential investment principles, practical long-term strategies, and insights into the profitable mutual fund investments and secrets to wealth-building.

Here is an extract of one mutual fund page 63: **Global Small/Mid-Cap** mutual fund. Investing $10,000 into a portfolio, the asset investment growth in five years is $30,695.38 209.65%. The mutual annualized performance of investment returns 41.93%.

Mutual Fund Investing begins with an exploration of fundamental investment concepts by helping readers understand financial markets, asset classes, and risk management. The objective is to emphasize the importance of creating personalized investment plans that are tailored to individual goals, risk tolerance, and time horizons. Readers will learn to set realistic objectives, diversify portfolios, and adjust strategies to changing market conditions.

The book details various investment strategies for different market environments, including bull and bear markets and periods of uncertainty. It includes case studies and real-life scenarios to illustrate strategies to ensure that even novice investors can grasp the essentials of investing in mutual funds.

TABLE OF CONTENTS:

RETIREMENT MANAGEMENT
INDIVIDUAL RETIREMENT ACCOUNT

Mutual Fund Investing

Investing in Individual Retirement Accounts (IRAs) is an excellent way for wage earners to build their retire-ment savings. It is important to start planning and preparing for retirement in advance. Various goals can be included in the investment strategy. Mutual fund investors select the goal that best aligns with their desired financial returns. There are three types of goals to choose from:

1. Aggressive goals are methods to achieve maximum returns. An aggressive investment strategy attempts to grow assets above average compared to its industry or the overall market.

2. Conservative goals are investment strategies that grow capital over the long-term. This type of fund has a minimal asset turno v e r or a high percentage of fixed assets and uses a buy-hold

investment strategy.

3. Moderate goals are investments that attempt to reduce risks and increase returns equally. The investment may incur a short-term loss of principal and the lower degree of liquidity in exchange for long-term appreciation.

Being successful in achieving financial goals requires committing and persevering to the goals pursuing.

Commitment is committing to the money saved and investing it into the retirement portfolio. After making the minimum investment and being a shareholder of the mutual fund, you can always make additional purchases.

Perseverance is making every effort, despite any unexpected financial difficulty, to save money for committed investments. Once the crisis passes, continue investing a s o r i g i n a l l y planned.

The maximum investment that can be contributed to a traditional IRA or Roth IRA is $6,500 for individuals under the age of 50. For individuals 50 years of age or older the maximum contribution is $7,500.

Maximizing your annual performance of investments is achieved when you reinvest all distribution of dividends are reinvested annually.

INVESTMENT PERFORMANCE

Mutual Funds

Profitable mutual funds, which are measured by mutual funds' making money for you, are priority investments for both short-term and long-term assets in building wealth! To accomplish management success requires: (1) being aware of the funds' net asset value changes; (2) tracking the funds' yield, amount of income the fund pays out; and (3) viewing its total annual return and performance.

Mutual funds are pooled investments managed by professional money managers. The money managers trade on exchanges and provide an accessible way for investors to get access to a wide mix of assets that are selected for the fund.

A mutual fund is an investment vehicle that invests investor's money to purchase a diversified portfolio of stocks, bonds, or other securities (stated strategy). All individual investors gain exposure to professionally managed port-folios and potentially benefit from market economic changes.

Here is some of the essential information included for each of the twenty-nine mutual fund reports. The information in the reports provide the reader with each unique profitable mutual fund investment:

1. Mutual Fund Investment Category
2. Investment Portfolio Style
3. Mutual Fund Name & Ticker Symbol
4. Contact (800 number, address, website)
5. Mutual Fund Details
6. Top 10 Major Holdings
7. Mutual Fund Annual Performance Returns
8. 3-year, 5-year, 10-year Annualized Return
9. Mutual fund Category Rank
10. Prosperity and Growth of $10,000 investment

for five-years. In addition, the mutual fund reports contain basic investment information:

ANNUALIZED PERFORMANCE: Annual mutual fund performance for each of 3-years, 5-years, and 10-years.

BETA: Mutual fund measurement of its volatility. The stock market's beta is always 1.0 and the money market fund's beta is always 0. The beta compares the fund risk to the overall market risk.

CAPITAL GAINS: Distributions to mutual funds shareholders of net profits on the sale of securities held in the fund's portfolio.

CATEGORY RANK: Mutual fund performance rank compared to the total funds in a specific in-Vestment category.

FRONT-END SALES FEE: the sales charge (per-centage) that investors pay when purchasing shares in a mutual fund.

INVESTMENT CATEGORY: Mutual funds are assigned to a specific investment objective group by Lipper Analytic analysts. The group is based on the investment policy statement from the fund's prospectus, and a review of the fund's investments.

INCOME DIVIDENDS: Distributions to mutual funds shareholders proof of interest and dividend income received on the securities held in the fund's portfolio.

INVESTMENT RISK: The profit loss can vary from low to high.

MUTUAL FUND AND TICKER SYMBOL: The name is the identification of the investment, and the symbol is a five-letter code assigned by NASDAQ to identify the mutual fund.

NET ASSET VALUE (NAV): the total market value of all assets of the mutual fund, plus all liabilities, divided by the number of shares outstanding. It is the price paid for each share purchased.

NO-LOAD FUND: Mutual fund that does not charge commission or sales charge when buying or selling the investment.

OPEN-END FUND: Mutual fund sells as many invested shares as investor request. Investor buys or sell trade shares through the mutual fund company directly.

TEN MAJOR HOLDINGS: A mutual fund's 10 largest investments represented by the percentage of the fund's net assets.

TOTAL NET ASSETS: Combined market value of the securities, cash and other assets of the mutual fund minus all liabilities.

TOTAL RETURN: Change in the investment value at end of date shown. The value includes the performance and reinvestment of dividend and capital gains distribution.

PROSPERITY AND GROWTH
Retirement/Savings Portfolio

An Individual Retirement Account (IRA) is one of the best types of accounts available when planning for retirement or savings. Owners of IRA accounts make all decisions on the investment's success. The investor manages and controls the assets in the investment. The investments can be aggressive, moderate, conservative, or a combination. The investors determine the amount of money to be invested and manage and select the moneymaking investments that are most profitable.

Traditional IRAs are a terrific way to save for the future! This type of account is "tax deferred" when all mutual fund income and capital gains distribution are reinvested. Taking this action the distribution is not taxable until you reach the age of 73.

Here are the Internal Revenue Service guidelines: https://www.irs.gov/retirement-plans/traditional-and-roth-iras

Starting in 2024, the maximum Traditional and Roth IRA purchase is $6,500 for individuals under 50 years of age or $7,500 if you are age 50 or older by the end of the year.

IRS Withholding Calculator helps determine the federal income tax withholding so your employer can

withhold the correct amount from your salary. This is especially helpful if you are starting a new job.

IRA Contribution at age 73 contributions to traditional IRA investments can no longer be made. However, you can still contribute to a Roth IRA and make rollover contributions to a Roth IRA.

IRA Required Minimum Distribution is the IRS required withdrawal of monies from the mutual fund portfolio. Compliance with the RMD is mandatory and may be subject to a 50% non-deductible federal excise tax. Tax Exempt: Investment income or capital gain distributions reinvested are tax exempt until 73 years of age.

IRS Withholding Calculator: This helps to determine the federal income tax withholding so your employer can withhold the correct amount from your salary.

Required Minimum Distribution: The Investor Government Required Minimum Distribution calculator determines the total dollar amount that must be withdrawn for the year of withdrawal. The total combined withdrawal from several of the IRA investments as long as the total withdrawals satisfy the required minimum for the year. Withdraws less than the RMD are subject to severe tax liability.

Retirement planning: Select mutual fund investments that provide above-average performance. The above average performance would be in the investment category. In addition, the performance since inception, should have more years of return gains and fewer return losses. Select the type of risk, minimal risk, average-risk, moderate-risk, or high-risk, that best achieves financial goals. Mutual fund investments can be purchased directly from the mutual fund.

Diversification is an effective method to increase wealth in personal or joint savings accounts, as well as retirement portfolios. It's a means to achieve primary goals of growing financial wealth over a short or long-term. The primary goal is not to maximize returns but limit the impact of volatility in a portfolio.

To create a diversified portfolio, the assets could consist of a mix of a low-risk mutual fund, an average-risk mutual fund, and a high-risk mutual fund and a certificate of deposit. Of course, the combined performance return should be above average. The 29 profitable mutual funds, in this book, include assets that the annual performance gain exceeds the average performance in all 29 investment categories.

MUTUAL FUND INVESTMENTS
30 FUNDS & CATEGORIES

ALTERNATIVE GLOBAL MACRO

Portfolio Style: Category

Investment Policy: See the fund prospectus.

Macquarie Asset Strategy Fund A - WASAX

800-523-1918

Macquarie Asset Strategy Fund A

6300 Lamar Avenue

Overland, KS 66202

FUND DETAILS:

Open-end fund

Beta: 0.99

Risk: high

Minimum Investment Purchase: $1,000

Front End Sales: 5.75%

Net Expense Ratio: 1.06%
Inception Date: July 10, 2000
Number of Years of Gains: 15
Number of Years of Losses: 8
Total Net Assets: $1.7 Billion

TOP 10 MAJOR HOLDINGS:

Microsoft Corporation
NVIDA Corporation
Alphabet Incorporated
Amazon.com Incorporated
Apple Incorporated
Taiwan Semiconductor Manufacturing Co Limited
MasterCard Incorporated
Salesforce, Incorporated
Home Depot
Eli Lilly & Company

FIVE-YEAR RETURNS:

Year: 2024
Net Asset Value: $21.29 5.55%
Dividend Distribution: $1.57 7.78% (reinvested)
Total Return: 13.33%

Year: 2023
Net Asset Value: $20.17 12.37%
Dividend Distribution: $0.58 3.24% (reinvested)
Total Return: 15.61%

Year: 2022
Net Asset Value: $17.95 -26.5%
Dividend Distribution: $3.20 13.1% (reinvested)
Total Return: -13.40%

Year: 2021
Net Asset Value: $24.43 2.0%
Dividend Distribution: $2.81 11.7% (reinvested)
Total Return: 13.70%

Year: 2020

Net Asset Value: $23.95 9.3%
Dividend Distribution: $0.64 2.9% (reinvested)
Total Return: 12.2%

SHARES INCREASED:

1-year 7.58%

3-Years 23.92% accumulative
5-Years 38.52% accumulative

MUTUAL FUND RETURNS:

1-year Return: 13.33%
Average Category Return: 7.03%
Rank: 7

3-year Annualized Return: 5.18%
Average Category Return: 1.80%
Rank: 28

5-year Annualized Return: 8.29%
Average Category Return: 4.58%
Rank: 6

10-year Annualized Return: 5.67%
Average Category Return: 3.52%
Rank: 8

Mutual fund $10,000 portfolio asset growth in five years:

2024 **$14,474.70**   13.33%
2023 $12,772.20   15.61%
2022 $11,047.60   -13.40%
2021 $12,757.10   13.70 %
2020 $11,200.00   12.20 %

Investment Category Average:

2024 **$12,277.41**   7.03%
2023 $11,471.00   10.72%
2022 $10,360.40   -12.34%
2021 $11,818.90   11.31%
2020 $10,618.00   6.18%

$$$$$

ALTERNATIVE LONG/SHORT EQUITY

Portfolio Style: Category

Investment Policy: See the fund prospectus.

Federated Hermes MDT Market Neutral Fund - QAMNX

800-341-7400

Federated Hermes, Inc.

1001 Liberty Ave – Suite 2100
Pittsburg, PA 15222

FUND DETAILS:

Open-end fund
Risk: high
Beta: 0.03
Minimum Investment Purchase: $1,500
Front End Sales: 5.50%
Net Expense Ratio: 2.18%

Inception Date: September 30, 2008
Number of Years of Gains: 14
Number of Years of Losses: 2
Total Net Assets: $854.54 million

TOP 10 MAJOR HOLDINGS

Federated Hermes Government Obligations Fund
Veralto Corporation
Go Daddy, Inc. Class A
AbbVie, Inc.
Jackson Financial, Inc.
Spotify Technology S.A.
Vistra Corporation
AppLovin Corporation
Qualcomm, Inc.
Ameriprise Financial, Inc.

FIVE-YEAR RETURNS:

Year: 2024
Net Asset Value: $19.69 15.48%
Dividend Distribution: $1.01 5.92% (reinvested)
Total Return: 21.40%

Year: 2023
Net Asset Value: $17.05 -1.33%
Dividend Distribution: $2.03 11.74% (reinvested)
Total Return: 10.42%

Year: 2022
Net Asset Value: $17.28 -2.70%
Dividend Distribution: $3.69 20.78% (reinvested)
Total Return: 18.08%

Year: 2021
Net Asset Value: $17.76 30.30%
Dividend Distribution: $0.00
Total Return: 30.30%

Year: 2020
Net Asset Value: $13.63 -4.48%
Dividend Distribution: $0.09 0.47% (reinvested)
Total Return: -4.01%

SHARES INCREASED:

1-Year 5.92%

3-Years 38.44% accumulative
5-Years 68.27% accumulative

MUTUAL FUND RETURNS:

1-year Return: 17.32%
Average Category Return: 12.47%
Rank: 29

3-year Annualized Return: 10.40%
Average Category Return: 6.55%
Rank: 16

5-year Annualized Return: 10.09%
Average Category Return: 4.24%
Rank: 20

10-year Annualized Return: 6.36%
Average Category Return: 5.00%
Rank: 29

Mutual fund $10,000 portfolio asset growth in five years:

2024 **$15,865.20** 17.32%
2023 $13,523.02 4.71%
2022 $12,914.74 9.18%
2021 $11,828.85 23.23%
2020 $ 9,599.00   -4.01%

Investment Category Average:

2024 **$12,235.93** 8.55%
2023 $11,272.16 5.09%
2022 $10,726.20 5.86%
2021 $10,132.44 6.95%
2020 $ 9,474.00 -5.26%

$$$$$$

ALTERNATIVE MANAGED FUTURES

Portfolio Style: Category
Investment Policy: See the fund prospectus.

Campbell Systematic Macro A – EBSAX
888-838-0770

Rbb Fund Inc.
615 E. Michigan St.
Milwaukee, WI 53202

FUND DETAILS:

Open end fund
Risk: High
Beta: -0.34
Minimum Investment Purchase: $2,500
Front End Sales: 3.50%

Net Expense Ratio: 2.00%
Inception Date: March 1, 2013
Number of Years of Gains: 7
Number of Years of Losses: 4
Total Net Assets: $56.90 million

TOP 10 HOLDINGS:

There are no companies listed on the Internet. This information is only available on the prospectus.

FIVE-YEAR ANNUAL RETURNS:

Year: 2024
Net Asset Value: $9.64 8.44%
Dividend Distribution: $0.75 2.85% (reinvested)
Total Return: 11.29%

Year: 2023
Net Asset Value: $8.89 -3.47%
Dividend Distribution: $0.12 1.35% (reinvested)
Total Return: -2.12%

Year: 2022
Net Asset Value: $9.21 13.84%
Dividend Distribution: $1.39 17.18% (reinvested)
Total Return: 31.02%

Year: 2021
Net Asset Value: $8.09 1.76%
Dividend Distribution: $0.57 7.17% (reinvested)
Total Return: 8.93%

Year: 2020
Net Asset Value: $7.95 3.11%
Dividend Distribution: $0.00
Total Return: 3.11%

SHARES INCREASED:

1-year 2.85%
3-Years 21.38% accumulative
5-Years 28.55% accumulative

MUTUAL FUND RETURNS:

1-year Return: 11.29%
Average Category Return: 3.60%
Rank: 17

3-year Annualized Return: 13.26%
Average Category Return: 3.06%
Rank: 16

5-year Annualized Return: 10.36%
Average Category Return: 3.52%
Rank: 7

10-year Annualized Return: 3.78%
Average Category Return: 2.31%
Rank: 10

Mutual fund $10,000 portfolio asset growth in five years:

2024 **$17,523.58**   11.29%
2023 $15,745.87   -2.12%
2022 $16,086.92   30.60%

2021 $12,317.70   8.93%
2020 $10,311.00   3.11%

Investment Category Average:

2024 **$11,872.95** 6.55%
2023 $11,143.08 2.62%
2022 $10,858.59   0.01%
2021 $10,857.50 3.86%
2020 $10,454.00 4.54%

$$$$$$

CONVERTIBLE SECURITIES

Portfolio Style: Convertible Securities

Investment Policy: See the fund prospectus.

Fidelity Convertible Securities Fund - FCVSX

877-208-0098

Fidelity Convertible Securities
82 Devonshire St.
Boston, MA 02109

FUND DETAILS:
Open end fund
Risk: above average
Beta: 0.86
Minimum Investment Purchase: N/A
Front End Sales: no load
Net Expense Ratio: 0.72%

Inception Date: January 5, 1987
Number of Years of Gains: 29
Number of Years of Losses: 8
Total Net Assets: $1.57 billion

TOP 10 MAJOR HOLDINGS

Boeing Company
Bank of America Corp.
DHT Holdings Inc.
Apollo Global Management Inc.
Ares Management Corporation
NextEra Energy Inc.
Albermarle Corporation
Micro Strategy Inc
Hewlett Packard Enterprise Co
AES Corporation

FIVE-YEAR RETURNS:

Year: 2024
Net Asset Value: $34.36 5.91% (reinvested)
Dividend Distribution: $2.60 8.00%
Total Return: 13.91%

Year: 2023
Net Asset Value: $32.44 9.74%
Dividend Distribution: $0.50 1.68% (reinvested)
Total Return: 11.42%

Year: 2022
Net Asset Value: $29.56 -19.28%
Dividend Distribution: $1.13 3.09% (reinvested)
Total Return: -16.19%

Year: 2021
Net Asset Value: $36.62 -7.90%
Dividend Distribution: $7.42 18.66% (reinvested)
Total Return: 10.76%

Year: 2020
Net Asset Value: $39.76 26.02%
Dividend Distribution: $4.30 13.63% (reinvested)
Total Return: 39.64%

MUTUAL FUND RETURNS:

1-year Return: 13.91%
Average Category Return: 11.24%
Rank: 13

3-year Annualized Return: 3.05%
Average Category Return: 0.90%
Rank: 6

5-year Annualized Return: 11.91%
Average Category Return: 9.40%
Rank: 6

10-year Annualized Return: 8.45%
Average Category Return: 7.64%
Rank: 28

Mutual fund $10,000 portfolio asset growth in five years:

2024 **$16,451.79** 13.91%
2023 $14,442.80 11.42%
2022 $12,962.50 -16.19%
2021 $15,466.50 10.76%

2020 $13,964.00 39.64%

Investment Category Average:
2024 **$14,607.26** 11.24%
2023 $13,131.30   8.97%
2022 $12,050.40 -17.50%
2021 $14,606.60   4.40%
2020 $13,991.00 39.91%

$$$$$$

EQUITY INCOME
Portfolio Style: Equity Income
Investment Policy: See the fund prospectus.

FAM Dividend Focus Fund; Investor - FAMEX
800-932-3271

Fenimore Asset Management Trust
384 North Grand St. – P.O. Box 399
Cobleskill, NY 12043

FUND DETAILS:

Open-End fund
Risk: high
Beta: 0.94
Minimum Investment Purchase: $500
Front End Sales: no-load
Net Expense Ratio: 1.22%

Inception Date: April 1, 1996
Number of Years of Gains: 22
Number of Years of Losses: 6
Total Net Asset: $4.9 billion

TOP 10 MAJOR HOLDINGS:

Train Technologies.
Arthur J. Gallagher & Company
CDW Corporation
Stryker Corporation.
Broadridge Financial. Solutions, Incorporated.
Ross Stores, Incorporated
Microchip Technology, Incorporated.
Heico Corporation Class A
Cintas Corporation.
Entegris, incorporated.

FIVE-YEAR RETURNS:

Year: 2024
Net Asset Value: $55.50 4.14%
Dividend Distribution: $1.85 3.48% (reinvested)
Total Return: 7.62%

Year: 2023
Net Asset Value: $53.29 18.87%
Dividend Distribution: $0.37 0.83% (reinvested)
Total Return: 19.79%

Year: 2022
Net Asset Value: $44.83 -14.58%
Dividend Distribution: $.61 1.16% (reinvested)
Total Return: -13.42%

Year: 2021
Net Asset Value: $52.48 23.92%
Dividend Distribution: $.85 2.00% (reinvested)
Total Return: 25.92%

Year: 2020
Net Asset Value: $42.35 10.69%
Dividend Distribution: $0.96 2.51% (reinvested)
Total Return: 13.20%

SHARES INCREASED:

1-year 3.48%

3-Years   5.47% accumulative
5-Years   9.98% accumulative

MUTUAL FUND RETURNS:

1-year Return: 7.62%
Average Category Return: 14.06%
Rank: 74

3-year Annualized Return: 4.66%
Average Category Return: 5.35%
Rank: 58%

5-year Annualized Return: 10.62%
Average Category Return: 10.37%
Rank: 47%

10-year Annualized Return: 10.13%
Average Category Return: 8.30%
Rank: 12

Mutual fund $10,000 portfolio asset growth in five years:

2024	**$15,910.02**	7.62%
2023	$14,783.52	19.79%
2022	$12,341.20	-13.42%
2021	$14,254.10	25.92%
2020	$11,320.00	13.20%

Investment Category Average:

2024	**$15,779.06**	14.06%
2023	$13,834.00	16.00%
2022	$11,925.80	-14.01%
2021	$13,868.90	23.40%
2020	$12,390.00	12.39%

$$$$$$$

FLEXIBLE PORTFOLIO
Portfolio Style: Flexible Portfolio
Investment Policy: See the fund prospectus.

Teberg Fund -TEBRX

631-470 2621

Northern Lights Fund Trust III

17605 Wright St.

Omaha, NE 68130

FUND DETAILS:

Open end fund

Risk: high

Beta: 1.50

Minimum Investment Purchase $2,000

Front End Sales: no load

Net Expense Ratio: 1.97%

Inception Date: April 1, 2002

Number of Years of Gains: 16

Number of Years of Losses: 6

Total Net Assets: $42.50 million

TOP 10 MAJOR HOLDINGS:

Van Eck Semiconductor ETF

Invesco QQQ Trust

iShares Semiconductor ETF

SPDR S&P 500 ETF Trust

SPDR Dow Jones Industrial Average ETF Trust

Berkshire Hathaway Incorporated

iShares Core S&P Small-Cap ETF

iShares Russell 2000 ETF

First American Government Obligations Fund Cl X

Financial Select Sector SPDR Fund

FIVE YEAR RETURNS

Year: 2024

Net Asset Value: $24.29 18.84%

Dividend Distribution: $0.39 1.92% (reinvested)

Total Return: 20.76%

Year: 2023

Net Asset Value: $20.44 34.92%

Dividend Distribution: 0.00%

Total Return: 34.92%

Year: 2022
Net Asset Value: $15.15 -22.47%
Dividend Distribution: $0.00
Total Return: -22.47%

Year: 2021
Net Asset Value: $19.54 25.02%
Dividend Distribution: $0.00
Total Return: 25.02%

Year: 2020
Net Asset Value: $15.63 20.05%
Dividend Distribution: $0.07 0.56% (reinvested)
Total Return: 20.61%

SHARES INCREASED:

1-Year   1.92%
3-Years   1.92% accumulative
5-Years   2.48% accumulative

MUTUAL FUND RETURNS:

1-year Return: 20.76%
Average Category Return: 10.86%
Rank: 7

3-year Annualized Return: 11.07%
Average Category Return: 2.04%
Rank: 4

5-year Annualized Return: 15.77%
Average Category Return: 5,86%
Rank: 2

10-year Annualized Return: 9.09%
Average Category Return: 5.32%
Rank: 4

Mutual fund $10,000 portfolio asset growth in five years:

2024 **$19,047.23**   20.76%
2023 $15,772.80   34.92%
2022 $11,690.40   -22.47%
2021 $15,078.60   25.02%

2020 $12,061.00   20.61%

Investment Category Average:

2024 **$12,917.18**   10.86%
2023 $11,651.80   10.74%
2022 $10,521.70   -15.49%
2021 $12,450.30   13.36%
2020 $10,983.00   9.83%

$$$$$$$

GLOBAL GROWTH

Portfolio Style: Global

Investment policy: See the fund prospectus.

Columbia Select Global Equity Fund- IGLGX

612-671-4321

Columbia Funds Series Trust II
225 Franklin St.
Boston, MA 02110

FUND DETAILS:
Open end fund
Risk: above average
Beta: 1.13
Minimum Investment Purchase: $2,000
Front End Sales: no load
Net Expense Ratio: 1.25%
Inception Date: May 29, 1990

Number of Years of Gains: 23
Number of Years of Losses: 10
Total Net Assets: $643.6 million

TOP 10 MAJOR HOLDINGS:
Microsoft Corporation
MasterCard Incorporated
Linde PLC
Amazon.Com Incorporated
NVIDIA Corporation
Lam Research Corporation
Alphabet Incorporated
Keyence Corporation
Intuit Incorporated
Synopsys Incorporated

FIVE-YEAR ANNUAL RETURNS:

Year: 2024
Net Asset Value: $18.57 10.40%
Dividend Distribution: $1.16 6.95% (reinvested)
Total Return: 17.35%

Year: 2023
Net Asset Value: $16.82 19.12%
Dividend Distribution: $0.76 5.35% (reinvested)
Total Return: 24.47%

Year: 2022
Net Asset Value: $14.12 -28.14%
Dividend Distribution: $0.00
Total Return: -28.14%

Year: 2021
Net Asset Value: $19.65 12.87%
Dividend Distribution: $1.79 10.28% (reinvested)
Total Return: 23.15%

Year: 2020
Net Asset Value: $17.41 16.38%
Dividend Distribution: $1.52 10.18% (reinvested)
Total Return: 26.56

SHARES INCREASED:

1-year 6.95%

3-Years   12.30% accumulative
5-Years   32.36% accumulative

MUTUAL FUND RETURNS:

1-year Return: 17.35%
Average Category Return: 17.02%
Rank: 35

3-year Annualized Return: 4.56%
Average Category Return: 4.25
Rank: 48

5-year Annualized Return: 12.68%
Average Category Return: 11.65%
Rank: 43

10-year Annualized Return: 11.24%
Average Category Return: 10.07%
Rank: 19

Mutual fund $10,000 portfolio asset growth in five years:

2024 **$16,359.29**   17.35%
2023 $13,940.60   24.47%
2022 $12,000.00   -28.14%
2021 $15,585.80   23.15 %
2020 $12,656.00   26.56 %

Investment Category Average:

2024 **$15,616.67**   17.02%
2023 $13,345.30   23.64%
2022 $10,793.70   -27.90%
2021 $14,970.40   12,84%
2020 $13,267.00   32.67%

$$$$$$$

GLOBAL MULTI-CAP VALUE
Portfolio Style: Global

Investment policy: See the fund prospectus.

Vanguard Global Capital Cycles Fund
VGPMX
800-662-2739

Vanguard Group
P.O. Box 2600 - V26
Valley Forge, PA 19482

FUND DETAILS:
Open end fund
Risk: above average
Beta: 0.81
Minimum Investment Purchase: $3000
Maximum Front End Sales: no load
Net Expense Ratio: 0.44%
Inception Date: May 23, 1984
Number of Years of Gains: 23
Number of Years of Losses: 17

Total Net Assets: $1.48 billion

TOP 10 MAJOR HOLDINGS:

Barrick Gold Corporation

Glencore PLC

Anglo American PLC

Alibaba Group Holding Limited

Unilever PLC

Samsung Electronics Co. Ltd

Wells Fargo & Co.

BWX Technologies, Inc.

Taiwan Semiconductor Manufacturing Co. Ltd. ADR

Novartis AG

FIVE-YEAR ANNUAL RETURNS:

Year: 2024

Net Asset Value: $12.63 3.02

Dividend Distribution: $0.34. 2.75% (reinvested)

Total Return: 5.79%

Year: 2023

Net Asset Value: $12.26 6.61%
Dividend Distribution: $0.39 3.42% (reinvested)
Total Return: 10.03%

Year: 2022
Net Asset Value: $11.50 3.98%
Dividend Distribution: $0.38 3.41% (reinvested)
Total Return: 7.39%

Year: 2021
Net Asset Value: $11.06 15.69%
Dividend Distribution: $0.36 3.80% (reinvested)
Total Return: 19.49%

Year: 2020
Net Asset Value: $9.56 14.77%
Dividend Distribution: $0.20 2.44% (reinvested)
Total Return: 17.21%

SHARES INCREASED:

1-Year   2.75%
3-Years   9.58% accumulative

5-Years   15.82% accumulative

MUTUAL FUND RETURNS:

1-year Return: 5.79%
Average Category Return: 10.41%
Rank: 80

3-year Annualized Return: 7.74%
Average Category Return: 5.65%
Rank: 14

5-year Annualized Return: 11.98%
Average Category Return: 7.44%
Rank: 1

10-year Annualized Return: 5.64%
Average Category Return: 6.66%
Rank: 80

Mutual fund $10,000 portfolio asset growth in five years:

2024 **$17,507.08**   5.79%
2023 $16,548.90   10.03%
2022 $15,040.40   7.39%
2021 $14,005.40   19.49%
2020 $11,721.00   17.21 %

Investment Category Average:

2024 **$14,024.50**   10.41%
2023 $12,702.20   15.05 %
2022 $11,040.60   -8.50%
2021 $12,066.30   17.72%
2020 $10,250.00   2.50%

$$$$$$

GLOBAL SMALL/MID-CAP
Portfolio Style: Global
Investment Policy: See the fund prospectus.

Kinetics Spin-Off/Corporation Restructuring Fund-LSHEX
800-930-3828

Kinetics Mutual Funds Inc.
555 Taxter Road, Suite 175
Sleepy Hollow, NY 10591

FUND DETAILS:

Open end fund
Risk: High
Beta: 0.84
Minimum Investment Purchase: $2,500
Front-End Sales Load: no load
Net Expense Ratio: 1.58%
Inception Date: December 11, 2017
Number of Years of Gains: 11

Number of Years of Losses: 6
Total Net Assets: $10.7 million

TOP 10 MAJOR HOLDINGS:
Texas Pacific Land Corporation
CSW Industries, Incorporated
Landbridge Co. LLC
Associated Capital Group, Incorporated
GAMCO Investors, Incorporated
Civeo Corporation
Liberty Media Corporation Series A
Prairie Sky Royalty Limited
Bakkat Holdings Inc.
Howard Hughes Holdings, Inc.

FIVE-YEAR ANNUAL RETURNS:

Year: 2024
Net Asset Value: $33.92   74.31%
Dividend Distribution: $1.60   8.22% (reinvested)
Total Return: 82.53%

Year 2023

Net Asset Value: $19.46   -26.09%
Dividend Distribution: $1.74   6.61% (reinvested)
Total Return: -19.48%

Year: 2022
Net Asset Value: $26.33   37.14%
Dividend Distribution: $0.44 2.29% (reinvested)
Total Return: 39.43%

Year: 2021
Net Asset Value: $19.20   42.75%
Dividend Distribution: $0.02   0.15% (reinvested)
Total Return: 42.90%

Year: 2020
Net Asset Value: $13.45 4.83%
Dividend Distribution: $0.08   0.62% (reinvested)
Total Return: 5.45%

SHARES INCREASED:
1-Year   8.22%
3-Years 17.12% accumulative
5-Years 17.89% accumulative

MUTUAL FUND RETURNS:

1-year Return: 82.53%
Average Category Return: 10.40%
Rank: 3

3-year Annualized Return: 34.16%
Average Category Return: 1.49%
Rank: 3

5-year Return: Annualized 30.%
Average Category Return: 11.36%
Rank: 3

10-year Annualized Return: 15.50%
Average Category Return: 7.86%
Rank: 9

Mutual fund $10,000 portfolio asset growth in five years:

2024 **$30,879.69**   82.53%
2023 $16,917.60   -19.48%

2022	$21,010.43	39.43%
2021	$15,068.80	42.90%
2020	$10,545.00	5.45%

Investment Category Average:

2024	**$15,338.09**	10.40%
2023	$13,893.20	21.37%
2022	$11,447.00	-27.29%
2021	$15,743.00	13.05%
2020	$13,926.00	39.26%

$$$$$$$

LARGE-CAP CORE

Portfolio Style: Growth & Income

Investment Policy: See the fund prospectus.

Vanguard Growth Income Fund-VQNPX

800-662-2739

The Vanguard Group

PO Box 7800

Philadelphia, PA 19101-9892

FUND DETAILS:

Open end fund

Risk: Average

Beta: 0.99

Minimum Investment Purchase: $3,000

Front-End Sales Load: no load

Net Expense Ratio: 0.35%

Inception Date: December 10, 1986

Number of Years of Gains: 30
Number of Years of Losses: 8
Total Net Assets: $3.69 billion

TOP 10 MAJOR HOLDINGS
Microsoft Corporation
NVIDIA Corporation
Apple, Inc
Amazon.com, Inc.
Alphabet, Inc.
Broadcom, Inc
Meta Platforms, Incorporated
Eli Lilly & Company
Merrick & Company, Inc.
Eli Lilly & Company

FIVE-YEAR ANNUAL RETURNS:

Year: 2024
Net Asset Value: $62.49 13.02%
Dividend Distribution: $7.26 13.14% (reinvested)
Total Return: 26.16%

Year: 2023

Net Asset Value: $55.29 14.71%
Dividend Distribution: $4.63 9.61% (reinvested)
Total Return: 24.32%

Year: 2022
Net Asset Value: $48.20 -24.57%
Dividend Distribution: $4.67 7.31% (reinvested)
Total Return: -17.26%

Year: 2021
Net Asset Value: $63.90 11.29%
Dividend Distribution: $9.69 16.88%(reinvested)
Total Return: 28.17%

Year: 2020
Net Asset Value: $57.42 10.47%
Dividend Distribution: $3.75 7.21% (reinvested)
Total Return: 17.68%

SHARES INCREASED:
1-Year   13.14%
3-Years 30.06% accumulative
5-Years 54.15% accumulative

MUTUAL FUND RETURNS:

1-year Return: 26.16%
Average Category Return: 22.21%
Rank: 15

3-year Annualized Return: 11.07%
Average Category Return: 9.19%
Rank: 24

5-year Annualized Return: 15.83%
Average Category Return: 13.89%
Rank: 24

10-year Annualized Return: 12.92%
Average Category Return: 11.88%
Rank: 19

Mutual fund $10,000 portfolio asset growth in five years:

2024 **$19,589.12** 26.16%

2023 $15,527.20   24.42%
2022 $12,479.70   -17.26%
2021 $15,083.00   28.17%
2020 $11,768.00   17.68%

Investment Category Average:

2024 **$18,126.92**   22.21%
2023 $14,832.60   22.32%
2022 $12,126.10   -16.96%
2021 $14,602.70   26.07%
2020 $11,583.00   15.83%

$$$$$$

LARGE-CAP GROWTH
Portfolio Style: Growth
Investment Policy: See the fund prospects.

Rydex NASDAQ 100 Fund-RYATX

800-820-0888

Rydex Series Funds
9601 Blackwell Rd. Suite 500
Rockville, MD 20850

FUND DETAILS
Open end fund
Risk: high
Beta: 1.19
Minimum Investment Purchase: $2,500
Front End Sales Load: 4.75%
Net Expense Ratio: 1.51%
Inception Date: March 31, 2004
Number of Years of Gains: 17
Number of Years of Losses: 3
Total Net Assets: $110.0 million

TOP 10 MAJOR HOLDINGS

Apple, Incorporated
NVIDIA corporation
Microsoft Corporation
Broadcom, Inc.
Meda Platforms Inc.
Amazon.com, Inc.
Tesla, Inc.,
Alphabet, Inc.
Costco Wholesale Corporation
Alphabet, Inc. Class C

FIVE-YEAR ANNUAL RETURNS:

Year: 2024
Net Asset Value: $72.39 14.90%
Dividend Distribution: $5.79 9.19% (reinvested)
Total Return: 24.09%

Year: 2023
Net Asset Value: $63.00 52.95%
Dividend Distribution: $0.00 0.00%
Total Return: 52.95%

Year: 2022
Net Asset Value: $41.19 -39.42%
Dividend Distribution: $4.07 5.99% (reinvested)
Total Return: -33.43%

Year: 2021
Net Asset Value: $67.99 19.64%
Dividend Distribution: $3.37 7.81% (reinvested)
Total Return: 27.45%

Year: 2020
Net Asset Value: $56.83 39.77%
Dividend Distribution: $2.61 6.42% (reinvested)
Total Return: 46.19%

SHARES INCREASED:
1-Year   9.19%
3-Years   15.18% accumulative
5-Years   29.41% accumulative

MUTUAL FUND RETURNS:

1-year Return: 24.09%

Average Category Return: 29.81%
Rank: 81

3-year Annualized Return: 14.54%
Average Category Return: 11.86%
Rank: 47

5-year Annualized Return: 23.45%
Average Category Return: 18.56%
Rank: 15

10-year Annualized Return: 16.71%
Average Category Return: 14.40%
Rank: 7

Mutual fund $10,000 portfolio asset growth in five years:

2024 **$23,540.86**   24.09%
2023 $18,970.80   52.95%
2022 $12,403.30   -33.43%
2021 $18,631.90   27.45%
2020 $14,611.90   46.19%

Investment Category Average:

Year	Amount	Percent
2024	**$19,625.71**	29.81%
2023	$15,118.80	40.53%
2022	$10,758.40	-34.75%
2021	$16,488.00	21.36%
2020	$13,586,00	35.86%

$$$$$$$

LARGE-CAP VALUE

Portfolio Style: Growth & Income

Investment Policy: See the fund prospectus

Dodge & Cox Stock Fund - DODGX

800-621-3979

Dodge & Cox Funds
555 California St. – 40th Floor
San Francisco, CA 94104

FUND DETAILS:
Open end fund
Risk: high
Beta: 0.87
Minimum Investment Purchase: $2,000
Front-End Sales Load: no load
Net Expense Ratio: 0.80%
Inception Date: January 4, 1965
Number of Years of Gains: 45
Number of Years of Losses: 14
Total Net Assets: $65.87 billion

TOP 10 MAJOR HOLDINGS:

Fiserv, Inc.
Charles Schwab Corporation
RTX Corporation
Wells Fargo & Co.
Sanofi ADR
MetLife, Inc.
Johnson Controls International PLC
Occidental Petroleum Corporation
CVS Health Corporation
Microsoft Corporation

FIVE-YEAR ANNUAL RETURNS:

Year: 2024
Net Asset Value: $257.18 5.60%
Dividend Distribution: $21.70 8.91% (reinvested)
Total Return: 14.51%

Year: 2023
Net Asset Value: $243.55 12.91%
Dividend Distribution: $9.88 4.57% (reinvested)
Total Return: 17.48%

Year: 2022
Net Asset Value: $215.71 -12.05%
Dividend Distribution: $11.85 4.83% (reinvested)
Total Return: -7.22%

Year: 2021
Net Asset Value: $245.26 26.08%
Dividend Distribution: $10.99 5.65% (reinvested)
Total Return: 31.73%

Year: 2020
Net Asset Value: $194.52 0.39%
Dividend Distribution: $13.21 6.82% (reinvested)
Total Return: 7.21%

SHARES INCREASED:
1-Year   8.91%
3-Years   18.31% accumulative
5-Years   30.78% accumulative

MUTUAL FUND RETURNS:

1-year Return: 14.51%

Average Category Return: 13.67%
Rank: 46

3-year Annualized Return: 8.26%
Average Category Return: 6.13%
Rank: 26

5-year Annualized Return: 12.74%
Average Category Return: 9.34%
Rank: 11

10-year Annualized Return: 10.35%
Average Category Return: 8.36%
Rank: 5

Mutual fund $10,000 portfolio asset growth in five years:

2024	**$17,627.13**	14.51%
2023	$15,393.53	17.48%
2022	$13,103.11	-7.22%
2021	$14,122.77	31.73%
2020	$10,721.00	7.21%

Investment Category Average:

2024 **$15,726.36**   13.67%
2023 $13,835.10   13.47%
2022 $12,192.74   -6.90%
2021 $13.096.39 2 5.83%
2020 $10,408.00   4 .08%

$$$$$$

MID-CAP CORE
Portfolio Style: Mid-Cap
Investment Policy: See the fund prospectus.

Victory Sycamore Established Value Fund-VETAX
800-539-3863

Victory Portfolios
3435 Stelzer Rd. Suite 1000
Columbus, OH 43219

FUND DETAILS:
Open end fund
Risk: below average
Beta: 0.89
Minimum Investment Purchase: $2,500
Front End Sales: 5.75%
Net Expense Ratio: 0.90%
Inception Date: May 5, 2000
Number of Years of Gains: 19
Number of Years of Losses: 5
Total Net Assets: $1.37 billion

TOP 10 MAJOR HOLDINGS:

Alliant Energy Corporation

NNN REIT, Inc

Willis Towers Watson PLC

US Foods Holding Corporation

Crown Holdings, Inc.

Quest Diagnostics Incorporated

BJ's Wholesale Club Holdings

Target Corporation

Hartford Financial Services Group, Inc.

Camden Property Trust

FIVE-YEAR ANNUAL RETURNS:

Year: 2024

Net Asset Value: $45.93   -0.93%

Dividend Distribution: $5.01   10.80% (reinvested)

Total Return: 9.87%

Year: 2023

Net Asset Value: $46.36 3.71%

Dividend Distribution: $2.79   6.24% (reinvested)

Total Return: 9.95%

Year: 2022
Net Asset Value: $44.70 -9.90%
Dividend Distribution: $3.55 7.16% (reinvested)
Total Return: -2.74%

Year: 2021
Net Asset Value: $49.61 21.33%
Dividend Distribution: $4.02 9.83% (reinvested)
Total Return: 31.16%

Year: 2020
Net Asset Value: $40.89 2.10%
Dividend Distribution: $2.13 5.32% (reinvested)
Total Return: 7.42%

SHARES INCREASED:

1-Year   10.80%

3-Years   24.20% accumulative

5-Years   39.35% accumulative

MUTUAL FUND RETURNS:

1-year Return: 9.87%
Average Category Return: 12.46%

Rank: 74

3-year Annualized Return: 5.69%
Average Category Return: 4.25%
Rank: 31

5-year Annualized Return: 11.11%
Average Category Return: 9.18%
Rank: 20

10-year Annualized Return: 10.42%
Average Category Return: 8.30%
Rank: 8

Mutual fund $10,000 portfolio asset growth in five years:

2024	**$16,553.67**	9.87%
2023	$15,066.60	9.95%
2022	$13,703.20	-2.74%
2021	$14,089.20	31.16%
2020	$10,742.00	7.42%

Investment Category Average:

Year	Amount	Percent
2024	**$15,224.53**	12.56%
2023	$13,525.70	14.71%
2022	$11,791.20	-12.56%
2021	$13,484.90	24.86%
2020	$10,800.00	8.00%

$$$$$$

MID-CAP GROWTH

Portfolio Style: Mid-Cap

Investment Policy: See the fund prospectus.

Value Line Mid-Cap Focused Fund - VLIFX

800-243-2729

Value Line Funds
P.O. Box 219729
Kansas City, MO 64121-9729

FUND DETAILS:
Open end fund
Risk: low
Beta: 0.91
Minimum Investment Purchase: $1,000
Front End Sales: no load
Net Expense Ratio: 1.07%
Inception Date: February 28, 1950
Number of Years of Gains: 58
Number of Years of Losses: 16

Total Net Assets: $528.30 million

TOP 10 MAJOR HOLDINGS

Tyler Technologies, Inc.
HEICO Corporation
Monolithic Power Systems, Inc.
MSCI, Inc.
Waste Connections, Inc.
Fair Issac Corporation
Lennox International, Inc.
CDW Corporation
Gartner, Inc.
IQVIA Holdings, Inc.

FIVE-YEAR ANNUAL RETURNS:

Year: 2024
Net Asset Value: $34.36 6.58%
Dividend Distribution: $.34 1.05% (reinvested)
Total Return: 7.63%

Year: 2023
Net Asset Value: $32.24 22.07%
Dividend Distribution: $0.01 0.04%(reinvested)
Total Return: 22.11%

Year: 2022
Net Asset Value: $26.41 -15.46%
Dividend Distribution: $1.90 6.08% (reinvested)
Total Return: -9.38%

Year: 2021
Net Asset Value: $31.24 10.43%
Dividend Distribution: $2.57 9.08% (reinvested)
Total Return: 19.51%

Year: 2020
Net Asset Value: $28.29 10.98%
Dividend Distribution: $2.21 8.67% (reinvested)
Total Return: 19.65%

SHARES INCREASED:
1-Year   1.05%
3-Years   7.17% accumulative
5-Years   24.92% accumulative

MUTUAL FUND RETURNS:

1-year Return: 7.62%
Average Category Return: 15.85%
Rank: 85

3-year Annualized Return: 6.78%
Average Category Return: 1.51%
Rank: 4

5-year Annualized Return: 11.90%
Average Category Return: 7.36%
Rank: 10

10-year Annualized Return: 12.73%
Average Category Return: 9.91%
Rank: 4

Mutual fund $10,000 portfolio asset growth in five years:

2024 **$17,028.82**   7.62%
2023 $15,823.10   22.11%
2022 $12,958.10   -9.38%
2021 $14,299.40   19.51%
2020 $11,965.00   19.65%

Investment Category Average:
2024 **$12,992.08**   12.85%

2023 $11,512.70   21.16%
2022 $ 9,502.10   -29.47%
2021 $13,472.40   12.27%
2020 $12,000.00   20.00%

$$$$$$

MID-CAP VALUE
Portfolio Style: Mid-Cap
Investment Policy: See the fund prospectus.

Hotchkis & Wiley Mid-Cap Value A-HWMAX
866-493-8637

Hotchkis & Wiley Funds
725 South Figueroa St. - 39th floor
Los Angeles, CA 90017-5439

FUND DETAILS:
Open end fund
Risk: high
Beta: 1.03
Minimum Investment Purchase: $2,500
Front End Sales: 5.25%
Net Expense Ratio: 1.20%
Inception Date: January 1, 2001
Number of Years of Gains: 17
Number of Years of Losses: 6
Total Net Assets: $117.10 million

TOP 10 MAJOR HOLDINGS

APA Corporation
Telefon AB L.M. Ericsson ADR
Citizens Financial Group, Inc
Kosmos Energy Ltd.
F5, Inc.
Popular, Inc.
Fluor corporation
State Street Corporation
Adient PLC
Magna International, Inc.

FIVE-YEAR ANNUAL RETURNS:

Year: 2024
Net Asset Value: $53.89 2.43%
Dividend Distribution: $0.53 1.01% (reinvested)
Total Return: 3.44%

Year: 2023
Net Asset Value:$52.61 19.49%
Dividend Distribution: $0.06 0.13% (reinvested)
Total Return: 19.62%

Year: 2022
Net Asset Value: $44.03 1.13%
Dividend Distribution: $0.13 0.29% (reinvested)
Total Return: 1.42%

Year: 2021
Net Asset Value: $43.54 37.31%
Dividend Distribution: $0.52 1.63% (reinvested)
Total Return: 38.94%

Year: 2020
Net Asset Value: $31.71 1.95%
Dividend Distribution: $0.71 2.20% (reinvested)
Total Return: 4.15%

SHARES INCREASED:
1-Year   1.01%
3-Years   1.43% accumulative
5-Years   5.26% accumulative

MUTUAL FUND RETURNS:

1-year Return: 3.44%
Average Category Return: 11.04%
Rank: 99

3-year Annualized Return: 8.16%
Average Category Return: 5.60%
Rank: 11

5-year Annualized Return: 13.51%
Average Category Return: 7.58%
Rank: 11

10-year Annualized Return: 6.03%
Average Category Return: 7.79%
Rank: 91

Mutual fund $10,000 portfolio asset growth in five years:

2024 **$18,159.41**   3.44%
2023 $17,555.50   19.62%
2022 $14,676.10   1.42%
2021 $14,470.60   38.94%
2020 $10,415.00   4.14%

Investment Category Average:

2024 **$14,163.37**   11.04%

2023	$12,755.20	12.40%
2022	$11,348.00	-6.65%
2021	$12,156.40	18.75%
2020	$10,237.50	2.37%

$$$$$$

MIXED TARGET ALLOCATION: CONSERVATIVE

Portfolio Style: Income

Investment policy: See the fund prospectus.

T. Rowe Price Spectrum Conservative Fund-PRSIX

800-638-5660

T. Rowe Price Funds

100 East Pratt St.

Baltimore, MD 21202

FUND DETAILS:

Open end fund

Risk: below low average

Beta: 0.50

Minimum Investment Purchase: $2,500

Front-End Sales: no load

Net Expense Ratio: 0.38%

Inception Date: July 29, 1994

Number of Years of Gains: 26

Number of Years of Losses: 4
Total Net Assets: $984.700 million

TOP 10 MAJOR HOLDINGS:
Price Multi Strategy Total Return Fund I Class
T. Rowe Price Dynamic Global Fund I
Price International Bond Fund USD Hedged I Cl
Price Emerging Markets Bond Fund I Cl
T. Rowe Price Institutional High Yield Fund
T. Rowe Price Treasury Reserve Fund
T. Rowe Price Real Assets Fund I
T. Rowe Price Institut Emerging Mkts Equity
T. Rowe Price Institutional Floating Rate Fund
Microsoft Corporation

FIVE-YEAR ANNUAL RETURNS:

Year: 2024
Net Asset Value: $19.64 4.41%
Dividend Distribution: $0.78   4.15% (reinvested)
Total Return: 8.56%

Year:2023
Net Asset Value: $18.81 7.73%
Dividend Distribution: $0.74 4.23% (reinvested)
Total Return: 11.96%

Year: 2022
Net Asset Value: $17.46   -18.22%
Dividend Distribution: $0.98 4.59% (reinvested)
Total Return: -13.63%

Year: 2021
Net Asset Value: $21.35 -0.56%
Dividend Distribution: $1.63 7.59% (reinvested)
Total Return: 7.03%

Year: 2020
Net Asset Value: $21.47 7.46%
Dividend Distribution: $0.81 4.05% (reinvested)
Total Return: 11.51%

SHARES INCREASED:
1-Year   4.15%
3-Years   12.97% accumulative
5-Years   24.61% accumulative

MUTUAL FUND RETURNS:

1-year Return: 8.56%
Average Category Return: 6.63%
Rank: 18

3-year Annualized Return: 2.30%
Average Category Return: 0.58%
Rank: 12

5-year Annualized Return: 5.09%
Average Category Return: 2.83%
Rank: 11

10-year Annualized Return: 5.33%
Average Category Return: 3.68%
Rank: 1

Mutual fund $10,000 portfolio asset growth in five years:

2024 **$12,528.91**   8.56%
2023 $11,541.00   11.96%
2022 $10,308.20   -13.63%
2021 $11,934.90   7.03%
2020 $11,150.00   11.51%

Investment Category Average:

2024 **$11,277.38**   6.63%
2023 $10,576.18   9.32%
2022 $ 9,674.52 -14.22%
2021 $11,278.29   5.81%
2020 $10,659.00   6.59%

$$$$$$

MIXED-ASSET: TARGET ALLOCATION GROWTH

Portfolio Style: Growth & Income

Investment Policy: See the fund prospectus

Value Line Capital Appreciation Fund -VALIX

800-243-2729

Value Line Funds
P.O. Box 219729
Kansas City, MO 64121-9729

FUND DETAILS:

Open end fund

Risk: high

Beta: 1.09

Minimum Investment Purchase: $1,000

Front End Sales: no load

Net Expense Ratio: 1.10%

Inception Date: October 1, 1952

Number of Years of Gains: 53

Number of Years of Losses: 1 9
Total Net Assets: $376.90 million

TOP 10 MAJOR HOLDINGS:

State Street Institutional U.S. Government Money Market
Meta Platforms, Inc.
NVIDIA Corporation
Apple, Inc.3
MicroStrategy, Inc.
Alphabet Inc.
Amazon.Com, Inc.
Microsoft Corporation
Advanced Mico Advances, Inc.
Uber Technologies, Inc.

FIVE-YEAR ANNUAL RETURNS:

Year: 2024
Net Asset Value: $12.63 20.29%
Dividend Distribution: $0.09 0.94%   (reinvested)
Total Return: 21.23%

Year: 2023
Net Asset Value: $10.50 33.42%
Dividend Distribution: $0.08 1.02% (reinvested)
Total Return: 34.44%

Year: 2022
Net Asset Value: $7.87 -36.94%
Dividend Distribution: $0.87 6.97% (reinvested)
Total Return: -29.97%

Year: 2021
Net Asset Value: $12.48   -3.42%
Dividend Distribution: $1.34 10.39% (reinvested)
Total Return: 6.97%

Year: 2020
Net Asset Value: $12.90   25.85%
Dividend Distribution: $0.71 6.92% (reinvested)
Total Return: 32.77%

SHARES INCREASED:

1-Year   0.94%%
3-Years   8.93% accumulative
5-Years   26.24% accumulative

MUTUAL FUND RETURNS:

1-year Return: 21.23%
Average Category Return: 12.81%
Rank: 3

3-year Annualized Return: 8.56%
Average Category Return: 4.36
Rank: 2

5-year Annualized Return: 13.09%
Average Category Return: 8.18%
Rank: 5

10-year Annualized Return: 9.67%
Average Category Return: 7.23
Rank: 4

Mutual fund $10,000 portfolio asset growth in five years:

2024 **$16,210.91**   21.23%
2023 $13,372.03   34.44%

2022 $ 9,946.47   -29.97%
2021 $14,203.15   6.97%
2020 $13,277.70   32.77%

Investment Category Average:

2024 **$14,328.45**   12.81%
2023 $12,701.40   15.56%
2022 $10,991.20   -15.30%
2021 $12,976.60   15.00%
2020 $11,284.00   12.84%

$$$$$$

MIXED-ASSET: TARGET ALLOCATION MODERATE

Portfolio Style: Income

Investment Policy: See the fund prospectus.

Janus Hendeson Balanced Fund T

877-335-2687

Janus Henderson Balanced T
151 Detroit Street
Denver, CO 80206

FUND DETAILS:
Open end fund
Risk: below average
Beta: 0.71
Minimum Investment Purchase: $2500
Front End Sales: no load
Net Expense Ratio: 0.82%
Inception Date: September 1, 1992
Number of Years of Gains: 27
Number of Years of Losses: 5

Total Net Assets: $4.51 billion

TOP 10 MAJOR HOLDINGS:
Microsoft Corporation
NVIDIA Corporation
Apple, Inc.
Alphabet, Inc.
Amazon.Com, Inc.
Meta Platforms, Inc.
Mastercard, Inc.
UnitedHealth Group, Inc.
Progressive Corporation
American Express Co.

FIVE-YEAR ANNUAL RETURNS

Year: 2024
Net Asset Value: $45.67 7.92%
Dividend Distribution: $3.10 7.32% (reinvested)
Total Return: 15.24%

Year: 2023
Net Asset Value: $42.32 12.68%
Dividend Distribution: $0.91 2.42% (reinvested)
Total Return: 15.10%

Year: 2022
Net Asset Value: $37.56   -18.19%
Dividend Distribution: $0.69 1.50% (reinvested)
Total Return: -16.69%

Year: 2021
Net Asset Value: $45.91 12.03%
Dividend Distribution: $1.01 2.46% (reinvested)
Total Return: 14.49%

Year: 2020
Net Asset Value: $40.98 11.36%
Dividend Distribution: $0.98 2.66% (reinvested)
Total Return: 14.02%

SHARES INCREASED:
1-Year   7.32%
3-Years   11.24% accumulative
5-Years   16.36% accumulative

MUTUAL FUND RETURNS:

1-year Return: 15.24%

Average Category Return: 9.25%
Rank: 6

3-year Annualized Return: 4.55%
Average Category Return: 3.99%
Rank: 14

5-year Annualized Return: 8.43%
Average Category Return: 6.22%
Rank: 6

10-year Annualized Return: 8.50%
Average Category Return: 5.41%
Rank: 3

Mutual fund $10,000 portfolio asset growth in five years:

2024	**$14,425.28**	15.24%
2023	$12,517.60	15.10%
2022	$10,875.41	-16.69%
2021	$13,054.15	14.49%
2020	$11,402.00	14.02%

Investment Category Average:

Year	Amount	Percent
2024	**$13,287.99**	9.25%
2023	$12,162.92	11.63%
2022	$10,895.74	-8.90%
2021	$11,960.20	16.22%
2020	$10,291.00	2.91%

$$$$$$$

MULTI-CAP CORE
Portfolio Style: Growth & Income
Investment Policy: See the fund Prospectus.

Centre American Select Equity - DHAMX
855-298-4236

Centre Funds
48 Wall Street
New York, NY 10005

FUND DETAILS:
Open end fund
Risk: below average
Beta: 0.84
Minimum Investment Purchase: $5000
Front End Sales: no load
Net Expense Ratio: 1.46%
Inception Date: December 21, 2011
Number of Years of Gains: 10
Number of Years of Losses: 1

TOTAL NET ASSETS: $269.9 million

TOP 10 MAJOR HOLDINGS:
iShares 20+ Year Treasury Bond ETT
NVIDIA Corporation
Microsoft Corporation
Apple, Inc.
Amazon.com, Inc.
Johnson & Johnson
International Flavors Fragrancies, Inc.
McCormick & Co., Inc.
Medtronic PLC
PepsiCo, Inc.
.

FIVE YEAR ANNUAL RETURNS:

Year: 2024
Net Asset Value: $15.20 -77.17%
Dividend Distribution: $1.90 7.05% (reinvested)
 Share Split: $22.54 84.01%
Total Return: 13.89%

Year: 2023

Net Asset Value: $15.00 12.02%
Dividend Distribution: $0.39 2.89% (reinvested)
Total Return: 14.91%

Year: 2022
Net Asset Value: $13.39 -4.63%
Dividend Distribution: $0.19 1.32% (reinvested)
Total Return: -3.31%

Year: 2021
Net Asset Value: $14.04 9.69%
Dividend Distribution: $2.27 17.70% (reinvested)
Total Return: 27.39%

Year: 2020
Net Asset Value: $12.80 25.12%
Dividend Distribution: $0.58 5.66% (reinvested)
Total Return: 30.78%

SHARES INCREASED:
1-Year 7.05%
3-Years 11.26% accumulative
5-Years 34.62% accumulative

MUTUAL FUND RETURNS:

1-year Return: 13.89%
Average Category Return: 18.87%
Rank: 74

3-year Annualized Return: 8.50%
Average Category Return: 7.37
Rank: 21

5-year Annualized Return: 16.73%
Average Category Return: 12.80%
Rank: 3

10-year Annualized Return: 12.00%
Average Category Return: 10.40%
Rank: 24

Mutual fund $10,000 portfolio asset growth in five years:

2024 **$21,081.49**   13.89%
2023 $18,510.40   14.91%
2022 $16,108.60   -3.31%
2021 $16,660.00   27.39%

2020 $13,078.00   30.78%

Investment Category Average:
2024 **$17,252.83**   18.87%
2023 $14,514.03   21.27%
2022 $11,968.36   -18.04%
2021 $14,602.69   26.07%
2020 $11,583.00   15.83%

$$$$$$$

MULTI-CAP GROWTH

Portfolio Style: Growth

Investment Policy: See the fund prospectus.

Schwartz Value Focus Fund-RCMFX

888-726 0753

Schwartz Value Focused Fund
c/o Ultimus Fund Solutions, LLC
135 Merchant St., Suite 230
Cincinnati, OH 45246

FUND DETAILS:
Open end fund
Risk: high
Beta: 0.91
Minimum Investment Purchase: $2,500
Front End Sales: no load
Net Expense Ratio: 1.26%
Inception Date: July 20, 1993
Number of Years of Gains: 31
Number of Years of Losses: 10
Total Net Assets: $52.40 million

TOP 10 MAJOR HOLDINGS:
Texas Pacific Land Corporation
LandBridge Co. Inc.
St. Joe Company
MasterCard, Incorporated
Occidental Petroleum Corporation
Madison Square Garden Sports Corporation
Schlumberger Limited
Moody's Corporation
Berkshire Hathaway, Inc.
Intercontinental Exchange, Inc.

FIVE-YEAR ANNUAL RETURNS:

Year: 2024
Net Asset Value: $52.73 20.58%
Dividend Distribution: $7.92 18.13% (reinvested)
Total Return: 38.71%

Year: 2023
Net Asset Value: $43.73 -1.33%
Dividend Distribution: $1.13 2.51% (reinvested)
Total Return: 1.18%

Year: 2022
Net Asset Value: $45.06 20.10%
Dividend Distribution: $0.39 1.05% (reinvested)
Total Return: 21.15%

Year: 2021
Net Asset Value: $37.52 22.86%
Dividend Distribution: $2.53 8.28% (reinvested)
Total Return: 31.14%

Year: 2020
Net Asset Value: $30.54 8.95%
Dividend Distribution: $0.75 2.67% (reinvested)
Total Return: 11.62%

SHARES INCREASED:
1-Year   18.13%
3-Years   21.69% accumulative
5-Years   32.64% accumulative

MUTUAL FUND RETURNS:

1-year Return: 38.71%

Average Category Return: 27.47%
Rank: 18

3-year Annualized Return: 20.35%
Average Category Return: 9.15%
Rank: 1

5-year Annualized Return: 20.76%
Average Category Return: 10.76%
Rank:

10-year Annualized Return:
Average Category Return:
Rank:

Mutual fund $10,000 portfolio asset growth in five years:

2024 **$24,888.73** 38.71%
2023 $17,943.00 1.18%
2022 $17,733.70 21.15%
2021 $14,637.80 31.14%
2020 $11,162.00 11.62%

Investment Category Average:

2024 **$14,717.18**   27.47%
2023 $11,545.60   32.89%
2022 $ 8,688.10   -32.92%
2021 $12,951.80   15.24%
2020 $11,239.00   12.39%

$$$$$$

MULTI-CAP VALUE

Portfolio Style: Growth & Income

Investment Policy: See the fund prospectus.

Oakmark Fund, Investor - OAKMX

800-625-6275

Harris Associates LP
111 South Wacker Drive - Suite 4600
Chicago, IL 60606

FUND DETAILS:

Open end fund

Risk: average

Beta: 1.04

Minimum Investment Purchase: $1000

Front End Sales: No load

Net Expense Ratio: 0.91%

Inception Date: August 5, 1991

Number of Years of Gains: 25

Number of Years of Losses: 8

Total Net Assets: $10.2 billion

TOP 10 MAJOR HOLDINGS:

Alphabet, Inc. Cl A

Fiserv, Inc.

Deere & Company

Citigroup, Inc.

Charles Schwab Corporation

General Motors Company

Intercontinental Exchange, Inc.

CBRE Group, Inc. Cl A

IQVIA Holdings, Inc.

FIVE YEAR ANNUAL RETURNS:

Year: 2024
Net Asset Value: $152.15 14.78%
Dividend Distribution: $1.64 1.24% (reinvested)
Total Return: 16.02%

Year: 2023
Net Asset Value: $132.56 29.57%
Dividend Distribution: $1.35 1.32% (reinvested)
Total Return: 30.89%

Year: 2022
Net Asset Value: $102.31   -14.15%
Dividend Distribution: $.94   0.79% (reinvested)
Total Return: -13.36%

Year: 2021
Net Asset Value: $119.17 26.47%
Dividend Distribution: $1.75 1.86% (reinvested)
Total Return: 28.33%

Year: 2020
Net Asset Value: $94.23 17.85%
Dividend Distribution: $0.15 0.19% (reinvested)
Total Return: 18.04%

SHARES INCREASED:
1-Year   1.24%
3-Years   3.35% accumulative
5-Years   5.40% accumulative

MUTUAL FUND RETURNS:

1-year Return: 16.02%

Average Category Return: 13.67%
Rank: 29

3-year Annualized Return: 11.18%
Average Category Return: 6.18%
Rank: 5

5-year Annualized Return: 15.98%
Average Category Return: 12.95%
Rank: 2

10-year Annualized Return: 11.77%
Average Category Return: 8.36%
Rank: 1

Mutual fund $10,000 portfolio asset growth in five years:

2024	**$19,930.38**	16.02%
2023	$17,178.40	30.89%
2022	$13,124.30	-13.36%
2021	$15,148.10	28.33%
2020	$11,804.00	18.04%

Investment Category Average:
2024 **$17,917.73** 13.67%
2023 $15,762.94 11.63%
2022 $14,120.70 -6.75%
2021 $15,142.80 26.19%
2020 $12,000.00 20.00%

$$$$$$$

SECTOR: FINANCIAL INSURANCE

Portfolio Style: Category

Investment Policy: See the fund prospectus.

Fidelity Select Insurance Portfolio - FSPCX

877-208-0098

Fidelity Select Portfolios

82 Devonshire Street

Boston, MA 02109

FUND DETAILS:

Open end fund

Risk: average

Beta: 0.75

Minimum Investment Purchase: NA

Front End Sales: no load

Net Expense Ratio: 0.73%

Inception Date: December 16, 1985
Number of Years of Gains: 31
Number of Years of Losses: 8
Total Net Assets: $944.70 million

TOP 10 MAJOR HOLDINGS:

Chubb Limited
Aon PLC
Arthur J Gallagher & Co.
Travelers Companies, Inc.
Marsh & McLennan companies, Inc.
Met Life, Inc.
Willis Towers Watson PLC
Progressive Corporation
The Hartford Financial Services Group, Inc.
American Financial Group, Inc

FIVE-YEAR RETURNS:

Year: 2024
Net Asset Value: $90.18 17.62%
Dividend Distribution: $8.28 10.80% (reinvested)
Total Return: 28.42%

Year: 2023
Net Asset Value: $76.67 3.54%
Dividend Distribution: $6.99 9.44% (reinvested)
Total Return: 12.98%

Year: 2022
Net Asset Value: $74.05 6.95%
Dividend Distribution: $0.56 0.81% (reinvested)
Total Return: 7.76%

Year: 2021
Net Asset Value: $69.24 18.43%
Dividend Distribution: $6.34 10.87% (reinvested)
Total Return: 29.30%

Year: 2020
Net Asset Value: $58.46 -9.60%
Dividend Distribution: $6.07 9.38% (reinvested)
Total Return: -0.22%

SHARES INCREASED:
1-Year   10.80%
3-Years   21.05% accumulative

5-Years   41.30% accumulative

MUTUAL FUND RETURNS:

1-year Return: 28.42%
Average Category Return: 25.36%
Rank: 46

3-year Annualized Return:
Average Category Return:
Rank: 3

5-year Annualized Return:
Average Category Return:
Rank: 5

10-year Annualized Return: 12.63%
Average Category Return: 6.52%
Rank: 8

Mutual fund $10,000 portfolio asset growth in five years:

2024	**$20,171.31**	28.42%
2023	$15,707.30	12.98%
2022	$13,902.70	7.76%
2021	$12,901.50	29.30%
2020	$ 9,978.00	-0.22%

Investment Category Average:

2024	**$14,884.29**	25.36%
2023	$11,873.24	10.96%
2022	$10,700.47	-15.43%
2021	$12,652.80	28.00%
2020	$ 9,885.00	-1.15%

$$$$$$$

SECTOR: HEALTH/ BIOTECHNOLOGY

Portfolio Style: Category

Investment   Policy: See the fund prospectus.

Fidelity Select Health Care Portfolio- FSPHX

877-208-0098

Fidelity Select Portfolios

82 Devonshire St.

Boston, MA 02/1/09

FUND DETAILS:

Open end fund

Risk: average

Beta: 0.70

Minimum Investment Purchase: N/A

Front End Sales: no load

Net Expense Ratio: 0.65%

Inception Date: July 14, 1981
Number of Years of Gains: 34
Number of Years of Losses: 9
Total Net Assets: $6.77 billion

TOP 10 MAJOR HOLDINGS:
United Health Group, Inc.
Boston Scientific Corp.
Eli Lilly & Company
Danaher Corporation
Penumbra, Inc.
Insulet Corporation
Masimo Corporation
Stryker Corporation
Argenx SE Sponsored ADR
Thermal Fisher Scientific, Inc.

FIVE-YEAR ANNUAL RETURNS:

Year: 2024
Net Asset Value: $27.25 -5.25%
Dividend Distribution: $2.93 10.18% (reinvested)
Total Return: 4.93%

Year: 2023
Net Asset Value: $28.76 4.13%
Dividend Distribution: $0.00
Total Return: 4.13%

Year: 2022
Net Asset Value: $27.62   -14.52%
Dividend Distribution: $0.55 1.70% (reinvested)
Total Return: -12.82%

Year: 2021
Net Asset Value: $32.31 1.80%
Dividend Distribution: $2.93 9.22% (reinvested)
Total Return: 11.02 %

Year: 2020
Net Asset Value: $31.74 % 10.98%
Dividend Distribution: $3.60 12.59% (reinvested)
Total Return: 23.57%

SHARES INCREASED:
1-Year   10.18%
3-Years   11.88% accumulative

5-Years   33.69% accumulative

MUTUAL FUND RETURNS:

1-year Return: 4.93%
Average Category Return: 1.34%
Rank: 25

3-year Annualized Return: -1.25%
Average Category Return: -3.53
Rank: 46

5-year Annualized Return: 6.17%
Average Category Return: 4.64%
Rank: 43

10-year Annualized Return: 8.22%
Average Category Return: 6.52%
Rank: 28

Mutual fund $10,000 portfolio asset growth in five years:

2024 **$12,939.65**   4.93%
2023 $12,331.69   4.13%
2022 $11,842.60   -12.82%
2021 $13,584.07   11.02%
2020 $12.235.70   23.57%

Investment Category Average:

2024 **$12,039.44**   1.34%
2023 $11,880.24   3.22%
2022 $11,509.63   -15.16%
2021 $13.566.28   6.88%
2020 $12.693.00   26.93%

$$$$$$$

SECTOR: S&P 500 INDEX

Portfolio Style: Category

Investment Policy: See the fund prospectus.

Fidelity 500 Index Fund -FXAIX
800-544-8544

Fidelity Select Portfolio
82 Devonshire St.
Boston, MA 02109

FUND DETAILS:
Open end fund
Risk: average
Beta: 1.01
Minimum Investment Purchase: N/A
Front-End Sales: no load
Net Expense Ratio: 0.02%
Inception Date: May 4, 2011
Number of Years of Gains: 11
Number of Years of Losses: 2
Total Net Asset: $619.45 billion

TOP 10 MAJOR HOLDINGS:

Apple, Inc.
NVIDIA Corporation
Microsoft Corporation
Amazon.com, Inc.
Meta Platforms, Inc.
Alphabet, Inc. Cl A
Tesla, Inc.
Berkshire Hathaway, Inc
Alphabet, Inc. Cl C
Broadcom, Inc.

FIVE YEAR ANNUAL RETURNS:

Year: 2024
Net Asset Value: $204.19 23.38%
Dividend Distribution: $2.68 1.62% (reinvested)
Total Return: 25.00%

Year: 2023
Net Asset Value: $165.49 24.32%
Dividend Distribution: $2.62 1.97% (reinvested)
Total Return: 26.29%

Year: 2022
Net Asset Value: $133.12   -19.48%
Dividend Distribution: $2.26 1.37% (reinvested)
Total Return: -18.11%

Year: 2021
Net Asset Value: $165.32 27.00%
Dividend Distribution: $2.02 1.55% (reinvested)
Total Return: 28.55%

Year: 2020
Net Asset Value: $130.17 16.20%(reinvested)
Dividend Distribution: $2.08 1.86%
Total Return: 18.06%

SHARES INCREASED:
1-Year   1.62%
3-Years   4.96% accumulative
5-Years   8.37% accumulative

MUTUAL FUND RETURNS:

1-year Return: 25.00%

Average Category Return: 24.51%
Rank: 6

3-year Annualized Return: 11.05%
Average Category Return: 10.96%
Rank: 3

5-year Annualized Return: 15.96%
Average Category Return: 13.75%
Rank: 6

10-year Annualized Return: 13.09%
Average Category Return: 12.61%
Rank: 3

Mutual fund $10,000 portfolio asset growth in five years:

2024	**$19,619.31**	25.00%
2023	$15,695.45	26.29%
2022	$12,428.10	-18.11%
2021	$15,176.60	28.55%
2020	$11,806.00	18.06%

Investment Category Average:

2024 **$18,023.11**   21.51%
2023 $14,832.61   22.32%
2022 $12,126.07   -16.96%
2021 $14,602.69   26.07%
2020 $11,583.00   15.83%

$$$$$$$

SECTOR: SCIENCE & TECHNOLOGY

Portfolio Style: Category

Investment Policy: See the fund prospectus.

Fidelity Select Semiconductors Portfolio-FSELX

877-208-0098

Fidelity Investments

P.O. Box 5000
Cincinnati, OH 45273-8610

FUND DETAILS:

Open end fund

Risk: high

Beta: 1.88

Minimum Investment Purchase: NA

Front End Sales: no load

Net Expense Ratio: 0.65%

Inception Date: July 29, 1985

Number of Years of Gains: 28

Number of Years of Losses: 11
Total Net Assets: $20.59 billion

TOP 10 MAJOR HOLDINGS:
NVIDIA Corporation
Broadcom, Inc.
ON Semiconductor Corporation
NXP Semiconductors N.V.
Marvel Technology Inc.
Taiwan Semiconductor Manufacturing Co. Ltd
Micron Technology, Inc.
GlobalFoundries, Inc.
Lam Research Corporation
Monolithic Power Systems, Inc.

FIVE YEAR ANNUAL RETURNS:

Year: 2024
Net Asset Value: $33.47 38.02%
Dividend Distribution: 1.33% 5.49% (reinvested)
Total Return: 43.51%

Year: 2023

Net Asset Value: $24.25 65.98%
Dividend Distribution: $1.78 12.16% (reinvested)
Total Return: 78.14%

Year: 2022
Net Asset Value: $14.61 -38.72%
Dividend Distribution: $0.98 4.11% (reinvested)
Total Return: -34.61%

Year: 2021
Net Asset Value: $23.84 46.98%
Dividend Distribution: $1.67 10.30% (reinvested)
Total Return: 57.28%

Year: 2020
Net Asset Value: $16.22 29.55%
Dividend Distribution: $1.32 10.54% (reinvested)
Total Return: 40.09%

SHARES INCREASED:
1-Year   5.49%
3-Years   21.76% accumulative
5-Years   42.60% accumulative

MUTUAL FUND RETURNS:

1-year Return: 43.51%
Average Category Return: 28.20%
Rank: 8

3-year Annualized Return: 29.01%
Average Category Return: 12.29%
Rank: 3

5-year Annualized Return: 36.88%
Average Category Return: 26.55%
Rank: 2

10-year Annualized Return: 25.99%
Average Category Return: 16.75%
Rank: 1

Mutual fund $10,000 portfolio asset growth in five years:

2024 **$36,832.85**   43.51%
2023 $25,665.70   78.14%

2022 $14,407.60   -34.61%
2021 $22,033.30   57.28%
2020 $14,009.00   40.09%

Investment Category Average:

2024 **$25,587.82**   28.20%
2023 $19,959.30   46.06%
2022 $13,665.20   -37.39%
2021 $21,825.80   55.91%
2020 $13,999.00   39.99%

$$$$$$

SECTOR: TELECOMMUNICATION

Portfolio Style: Category

Investment Policy: See the fund prospectus.

T. Rowe Price Communication & Technology Fund-PRMTX

800-225-5132

T. Rowe Price Media & Telecommunication
100 E Pratt St.
Baltimore, MD 21202

FUND DETAILS:
Open end fund
Risk: average
Beta: 1.16
Minimum Investment Purchase: $2,500
Front End Sales: no load
Net Expense Ratio: 0.77%

Inception Date: October 13, 1993
Number of Years of Gains: 23
Number of Years of Losses: 8
Total Net Assets: $5.66 billion

TOP 10 MAJOR HOLDINGS:
Meta Platforms, Inc.
Netflix, Inc.
Apple, Inc.
Alphabet, Inc.
Microsoft corporation
T-Mobile U.S., Inc.
Amazon. com, Inc.
NVIDIA Corporation
AT&T, Inc.
Mercado Libre, Inc.

FIVE YEAR ANNUAL RETURNS:

Year: 2024
Net Asset Value: $154.19   29.01%
Dividend Distribution: $10.89   9.11% (reinvested)
Total Return: 38.12%

Year: 2023
Net Asset Value: $119.52 29.15%
Dividend Distribution: $9.37 10.13% (reinvested)
Total Return: 39.28%

Year: 2022
Net Asset Value: $92.54   -49.32%
Dividend Distribution: $16.20 8.87% (reinvested)
Total Return: -40.45%

Year: 2021
Net Asset Value: $182.60 1.17%
Dividend Distribution: $15.25 8.45% (reinvested)
Total Return: 9.62%

Year: 2020
Net Asset Value: $180.49 45.84%
Dividend Distribution: $9.55 7.72% (reinvested)
Total Return: 53.56%

SHARES INCREASED:
1-Year   9.11%
3-Years   28.11% accumulative

5-Years   44.28% accumulative

MUTUAL FUND RETURNS:

1-year Return: 38.12%
Average Category Return: 25.54%
Rank: 9

3-year Annualized Return: 12.32%
Average Category Return: 4.98
Rank: 6

5-year Annualized Return: 20.03%
Average Category Return: 10.05
Rank: 13

10-year Annualized Return: 15.03%
Average Category Return: 6.83%
Rank: 8

Mutual fund $10,000 portfolio asset growth in five years:

2024	**$19,283.90**	38.12%
2023	$13,961.70	39.28%
2022	$10,024.20	-40.45%
2021	$16,833.20	9.62%
2020	$15,356.00	53.56%

Investment Category Average:

2024	**$14,118.23**	25.54%
2023	$11,246.00	23.21%
2022	$ 9,127.55	-33.82%
2021	$13,792.00	10.38%
2020	$12,495.00	24.95%

$$$$$$

King A. Kovacs

SMALL-CAP CORE
Portfolio Style: Small-Cap
Investment Policy: See the fund prospectus.

Auer Growth Fund - AUERX
888-711-2837

Auer Growth Fund
Unified Series Trust
2960 N. Meridian Street, Suite 300
Indianapolis, IN 46208

FUND DETAILS:
Open end fund
Risk: above average
Beta: 0.96
Minimum Investment Purchase: $2,000
Front End Sales: no load
Net Expense Ratio: 2.07%
Inception Date: December 28, 2007
Number of Years of Gains: 11
Number of Years of Losses: 6
Total Net Assets: $59.80 million

TOP 10 MAJOR HOLDINGS:

Fidelity Institutional Money Market Govt Portfolio

Catalyst Pharmaceuticals, Inc.

Goldman Sachs Group, Inc.

Amphastar Pharmaceuticals, Inc.

First Solar, Inc.

Hamilton Insurance Group Ltd.

General Motors company

Renaissance Re Holdings Ltd.

GRAVITY Company Ltd ADR

Castamere, Inc.

FIVE YEAR ANNUAL RETURNS:

Year: 2024
Net Asset Value: $13.34 -9.99%
Dividend Distribution: $3.16 21.30% (reinvested)
Total Return: 11.31%

Year: 2023
Net Asset Value: $14.82 15.78%
Dividend Distribution: $0.70 5.51% (reinvested)
Total Return: 21.29%

Year: 2022
Net Asset Value: $12.80   3.90%
Dividend Distribution: $.75 6.07% (reinvested)
Total Return: 9.97%

Year: 2021
Net Asset Value: $12.32   45.11%
Dividend Distribution: $0.00
Total Return: 45.11%

Year: 2020
Net Asset Value: $8.49   -1.85%
Dividend Distribution: $0.00
Total Return: -1.85%

SHARES INCREASED:

1-Year   21.30%
3-Years   32.88% accumulative
5-Years   32.88% accumulative

MUTUAL FUND RETURNS:

1-year Return: 11.31%

Average Category Return: 10.76%
Rank: 3

3-year Annualized Return:
Average Category Return:
Rank: 1

5-year Annualized Return:
Average Category Return:
Rank: 1

10-year Annualized Return: 9.09%
Average Category Return: 7.76%
Rank: 1

Mutual fund $10,000 portfolio asset growth in five years:

2024 **$21,145.67**   11.31%
2023 $18,997.10   21.29%
2022 $15,662.50   9.97%
2021 $14,242.50   45.11%
  2020 $ 9,815.00   -1.85%

Investment Category Average:

2024 **$14,261.57**   10.76%
2023 $12,876.10   15.57%
2022 $11,141.40   -14.43%
2021 $13,020.20   25.17%
2020 $10,402.00   4.02%

$$$$$$

SMALL-CAP GROWTH
Portfolio Style: Small-Cap
Investment category: See the fund prospectus.

Virtus KAR Small-Cap Fund – PKSAX
800-243 1574

Virtus Equity Trust
101 Munson St.
Greenfield, MA 01301

FUND DETAILS:
Open end fund
Risk: low
Beta: 0.99
Minimum Investment Purchase: $2500
Front End Sales: 5.50%
Net Expense Ratio: 1.27%
Inception Date: August 30, 2002
Number of Years of Gains: 18
Number of Years of Losses: 4

Total Net Assets: $184.80 million

TOP 10 MAJOR HOLDINGS:
EMCOR, Group, Inc
Simpson Manufacturing Company, Inc.
FTI Consulting, Inc.
Primerica, Inc.
Dreyfus Government Cash Management
Institutional Shares
CorVel Corporation
Acushnet Holdings Corporation
Kadant, Inc.
Moelis & Company
UFP Industries

FIVE YEAR ANNUAL RETURNS:

Year: 2024
Net Asset Value: $52.08%   8.89%
Dividend Distribution: $2.21   4.62% (reinvested)
Total Return: 13.51%

Year: 2023

Net Asset Value: $47.83 26.40%
Dividend Distribution: $2.12 5.60% (reinvested)
Total Return: 32.00%

Year: 2022
Net Asset Value: $37.84 -15.91%
Dividend Distribution: $2.68 5.88% (reinvested)
Total Return: -10.03%

Year: 2021
Net Asset Value: $45.54 4.81%
Dividend Distribution: $5.84 13.44% (reinvested)
Total Return: 18.25%

Year: 2020
Net Asset Value: $43.45 10.84%
Dividend Distribution: $3.39 8.75% (reinvested)
Total Return: 19.59%

SHARES INCREASED:
1-Year   4.62%
3-Years   16.10% accumulative
5-Years   38.29% accumulative

MUTUAL FUND RETURNS:

1-year Return: 13.51%
Average Category Return: 14.76%
Rank: 74

3-year Annualized Return: 17.10%
Average Category Return: 6.70%
Rank: 1

5-year Annualized Return: 17.83%
Average Category Return: 13.97%
Rank: 5

10-year Annualized Return: 15.31%
Average Category Return: 9.12%
Rank: 2

Mutual fund $10,000 portfolio asset growth in five years:

2024 **$21,349.64**   13.51%
2023 $18,808.60   47.83%

2022 $12,723.10   -10.03%
2021 $14,141.50   18.25%
2020 $11,959.00   19.59%

Investment Category Average:

2024 **$17,126.21**   14.76%
2023 $14,923.50   32.00%
2022 $11,306.00   -26.65%
2021 $15,413.30   11.40%
2020 $13,836.00   38.36%

$$$$$$$

SMALL-CAP VALUE
Portfolio Style: Small-Cap
Investment Policy: See the fund prospectus.

Invesco Small-Cap Value Fund-VSCAX
800-959-4246

Aim Sector Funds
11 Greenway Plaza, Suite 100
Houston, TX 77046

FUND DETAILS:

Open end fund
Risk: high
Beta: 0.99
Minimum Investment Purchase: $1000
Front-End Sales: 5.50%
Net Expense Ratio: 1.09%
Inception Date: June 21, 1999
Number of Years of Gains: 17

Number of Years of Losses: 6
Total Net Assets: $2.6 billion

TOP 10 MAJOR HOLDINGS:

Coherent Corporation
Western Alliance Bancorporation
Lumentum Holdings, Inc.
Vertiv Holdings Company
East West Bancorp Corporation
Rambus, Inc.
NRG, Inc.
Expedia Group, Inc.
Globe Life, Inc.
Webster Financial Corporation

FIVE-YEAR ANNUAL RETURNS:

Year: 2024
Net Asset Value: $23.51 15.75%
Dividend Distribution: $1.78 8.78% (reinvested)
Total Return: 24.53%

Year: 2023

Net Asset Value: $20.31 16.99%
Dividend Distribution: $1.02 5.92% (reinvested)
Total Return: 22.91%

Year: 2022
Net Asset Value: $17.36 -5.45%
Dividend Distribution: $1.79 9.77% (reinvested)
Total Return: 4.32%

Year: 2021
Net Asset Value $18.36 15.98%
Dividend Distribution: $3.25 20.53%(reinvested)
Total Return: 36.51%

Year: 2020
Net Asset Value: $15.83 10.47%
Dividend Distribution: $0.05 0.34% (reinvested)
Total Return: 10.81%

SHARES INCREASED:
1-Year   8.78%
3-Years   24.47% accumulative
5-Years   50.92% accumulative

MUTUAL FUND RETURNS:

1-year Return: 24.53%
Average Category Return: 9.82%
Rank: 4

3-year Annualized Return: 17.25%
Average Category Return: 5.87%
Rank: 2

5-year Annualized Return: 19.82%
Average Category Return: 10.78%
Rank: 2

10-year Annualized Return: 11.76%
Average Category Return: 7.58%
Rank: 3

Mutual fund $10,000 portfolio asset growth in five years:

2024 **$24,153.09** 24.53%
2023 $19,395.40 22.91%

2022 $15,780.10   4.32%
2021 $15,126.70   36.51%
2020 $11,081.00   10.81%

Investment Category Average:

2024 **$16,075.34**   9.82%
2023 $14,637.90   16.34%
2022 $12,582.00   -8.56%
2021 $13,759.80   32.28%
2020 $10,402.00   4.02%

$$$$$$

FACT FINDERS

Financial Internets:

Wall Street Journal
https://www.wsj.com/market-data/quotes

MORNINGSTAR
https://www.morningstar.com/funds

BARRON'S
https://www.barrons.com/market-data/funds

Yahoo! Finance
https://finance.yahoo.com/quote

Big Charts
https://bigcharts.marketwatch.com/historical

Individual Requirement Arrangements
https://www.irs.gov

Traditional IRAs/IRS
https://www.irs.gov/retirement-plans/

ABOUT THE AUTHOR

Mutual Funds Analyst:

King A. Kovacs an Analyst and Researcher, and Founder/CEO of Mutual Interest Data Service, Ltd.

Since 1999, he has researched thousands of mutual funds to identify moneymaking investments.

In 2024, he identified 30 profitable mutual funds, categorized by investment objectives. The objective? Assist investors in managing the growth of portfolio returns.

www.ingramcontent.com/pod-product-compliance
Lightning Source LLC
Chambersburg PA
CBHW030637220526
45463CB00004B/1551